HAYLEY WILLIAMS

Beyond the Music – A Life of Passion, Strength, and Artistry

Marilyn Clinton

Content

INTRODUCTION

The words "raw emotion," "unapologetic individuality," and "fierce determination" are all associated with Hayley Williams. Being the dynamic lead singer of Paramore and a successful solo performer, she has completely changed the perception of what it means to be a woman in the rock industry. However, it would be inaccurate to consider Hayley only as a rock star, given the scope of her life, impact, and personal development. The human tale hidden behind the microphone, the colorful hair, and the music videos are considerably more complex and profound than the image projected on stage. This is a tale of resilience, rebirth, and the strength of openness.

Early on, Hayley was just a Mississippi small-town girl from Meridian who was adjusting to the usual difficulties of puberty and the extra complications of relocating to a new metropolis at a young age. Even so, though, her love of music was evident. She had a deep connection to music and emotion that went beyond her years, and this connection was fueling the fire that would eventually define her craft. Her early musical tastes ranged from gospel to punk rock. They were varied and indicative of a young woman still searching for her identity in a society that frequently encourages uniformity.

When Hayley's family moved to Nashville, Tennessee, at thirteen, her life took a significant turn. Nashville has a rich musical history, and Hayley would use this city as the backdrop for her journey from a shy child with enormous goals to a teenage prodigy on the verge of success. She met the Farro brothers in Nashville, and the two went on to start the band Paramore, which would soon become an international sensation. However, the road to stardom was far from easy.

Hayley was frequently met with skepticism from the beginning. In the mid-2000s, female-fronted rock bands were still somewhat of a novelty, and Hayley was quickly singled out by reviewers who questioned her authenticity due to her age and gender. She remained unfazed, though. She rapidly demonstrated that she was more than just another pop-punk princess, possessing a formidable voice and an unwavering work ethic. While Paramore's first album, "All We Know Is Falling", made them famous, their follow-up, "Riot!", was the record that made them famous.

"Riot!" became a landmark album of the 2000s with its catchy hooks and powerful choruses, and hits like "Misery Business" made Hayley a household name. She was suddenly all over the place, appearing on magazine covers, performing on stages worldwide, and winning millions of followers with her unique style and attitude. However, Hayley was under increasing strain as Paramore's star grew. The pressures of being a young band frontwoman came with many responsibilities, and her idyllic life started to fall apart.

Behind the scenes, Hayley was juggling pressures from the industry, internal band disagreements, and the emotional toll of growing up in the spotlight. The Farro brothers' 2010 exits were especially devastating as

Hayley began to wonder about her place in the music business and Paramore's future. This would have been the tipping point for a lot of people. For Hayley, though, it was a wake-up call and an opportunity to reconsider who she was as a person and an artist.

A reflection and development phase ensued, ultimately shaping the latter phase of her existence. The band Paramore underwent a creative metamorphosis with the publication of their self-titled album in 2013, which included a fresh sound and a more mature lyrical viewpoint. Hayley's talent for combining appealing pop melodies with very personal themes was showcased in songs like "Ain't It Fun" and "Still Into You," the album's success demonstrated that Paramore was far from done. They were only beginning.

However, Hayley's personal life was falling apart even as the band did well. Her mental health was starting to suffer as a result of identity, anxiety, and depression struggles, which made her doubt everything she had accomplished. She was open in interviews about the strain to keep up an image that didn't necessarily represent who she was. She was the feisty, self-assured frontwoman on stage, but off it, she frequently felt alone and lost.

This was when Hayley bravely chose to leave Paramore's security and go out alone. "Petals for Armor", her debut solo album, was a stark and objective examination of pain, recovery, and self-discovery released in 2020. In addition to deviating from the energetic sound that fans had grown to love from Paramore, the album featured a very intimate portrayal of Hayley's inner life. Peeling back the layers of her public persona, songs like "Simmer" and "Dead Horse" showed a lady struggling with the complexity of her emotions.

"Petals for Armor" was more than simply an artistic project for Hayley; it was her lifeline. She was able to face the anguish she had been ignoring for years through the album-making process, and as a result, she gained a fresh perspective and direction. This phase of her life was a turning point in her professional and personal development. She started to see vulnerability as a strength rather than a weakness and utilized her position to inspire others to follow suit.

Nevertheless, Paramore played a significant role in Hayley's life even as she navigated the highs and lows of her solo career. "After Laughter", the band's album released in 2017, demonstrated Hayley's continued development as a vocalist and songwriter. The album's mix of cheerful pop with 80s influences and incredibly depressing lyrics reflected the duality that characterized Hayley's life: the contrast between her internal struggles and her public triumph.

Not only has Hayley developed as an artist over the years, but she has also grown and changed personally. She has become a mental health advocate, utilizing her experiences to spread the word and assist others in need. She has also accepted her position as a feminist icon and spoken out against the discrimination women experience in the music business and other fields.

Hayley Williams' resistance to being characterized by just one thing makes her alluring. In addition to being a musician, she is also an entrepreneur, a creative visionary, and—above all—a human person who doesn't mind owning her imperfections. Hayley has inspired countless followers with her willingness to be genuine and share her challenges as openly as her achievements in a culture that frequently expects perfection.

This book aims to examine the whole range of Hayley Williams' life, going beyond the headlines, the number-one hits, and the striking hair colors. This is a tale of resiliency, ingenuity, and the strength of self-expression—from her modest upbringing in Mississippi to the pinnacles of success with Paramore, from her lowest points to her creative and emotional rebirth. It's the tale of a woman who has made a lasting impression on the music industry and beyond by living unashamedly, truthfully, and on her terms.

CHAPTER 1: ROOTS OF RESILIENCE

Growing Up in Meridian: The Early Years

Meridian, Mississippi, is a sleepy little town in the heart of the American South, more famous for its railroad junction than for being the birthplace of rock stars. However, Hayley Williams' journey started in this sleepy, firmly conventional village. There were tiny houses along the streets and a strong sense of community and Southern hospitality in the air. Meridian was a supportive home, but it was also a place Hayley would soon outgrow for a girl with goals that stretched far beyond the limits of this town.

On December 27, 1988, Hayley was born into a close-knit family. The regularity of Southern life—church on Sundays, school on weekdays, and family time in between—shaped her upbringing as the youngest of three sisters. There was a combination of complexity and simplicity in Meridian's life. It was a town full of customs, everyone knew one another, and community was ingrained in daily life. However, Hayley sensed from an early age that her destiny lay elsewhere. Meridian was at home, but she couldn't quite fit the mold of small-town life, and she was restless, curious, and drawn to something greater.

The South's culture was deeply ingrained with music, permeating every aspect of daily life. In churches, neighborhood fairs, and family get-togethers, the sounds of gospel, country, and blues filled the air. For Hayley, music was more than background noise—it was a portal to another world and a means of escape. The sounds of gospel music filling their local church and the tunes her mother sang around the house highlighted her earliest memories. During services, she would sit with her eyes wide open, taking in all the emotion that radiated from the pulpit, the choir's energy, and the strength of their voices. In the quiet Meridian pews, Hayley initially realized the profound relationship between music and feeling—a revelation that would define her professional life.

Life was only sometimes peaceful. Even though living in a tiny village could appear ideal, there were drawbacks. When Hayley was a little child, her parents divorced, a situation that would have a lasting effect on her. Her sense of stability was utterly destroyed by her family's split, which, in many ways, accelerated her need for music as a coping technique. Following the incident, Hayley's mother, Cristi, emerged as a formidable force, providing her courage, resiliency, and unwavering love. Hayley's love of music was fostered by Cristi, who saw early on that her daughter possessed unique qualities. She developed as Hayley's biggest fan, frequently giving up her wants to drive her to nearby music lessons and performances.

However, the divorce also had an additional consequence, forcing Hayley to face feelings she didn't wholly comprehend. Her life began to feel confused, lonely, and depressed; these were feelings she would eventually express through her songs. She learned to rely on music as a haven, her go-to source when everything else felt too much. When Hayley was nine years old, she realized that the feelings she poured into her songs were a means of connecting with people who could be experiencing similar emotions. Even then, she was aware of the power of vulnerability and how music could reach places of the soul that words could not.

For Hayley, school in Meridian was a complex experience. She was an intelligent student but also had a rebellious streak from an early age. She wasn't willing to go along with the flow or meet demands. She frequently finds herself at odds with the strict curriculum because of her inventiveness and curiosity. Hayley was never the type of child to sit quietly for hours at a desk, lost in textbooks; instead, she was restless, and her thoughts were constantly drawn to songs and lyrics. While most children were happy to follow the daily lesson plan,

Hayley was already blazing her trail, which occasionally deviated from the norm.

Nevertheless, Hayley lived in Meridian with a small group of close friends. The village offered a sense of familiarity and comfort despite its small size. She spent her summers playing outside, riding her bike, and dreaming of a life that would stay rooted in the South for many of her contemporaries. Meridian, meanwhile, was never Hayley's ultimate objective. As a young child, she knew there was a world outside her small village, and she naturally desired to explore it. She was aware that music was her escape.

When Hayley was a preteen, everyone in her immediate vicinity could tell she wasn't like other kids in Meridian. Her sense of style, already inclined toward the audacious and out of the ordinary, distinguished her as her voice developed. While other youngsters were satisfied listening to mainstream radio tunes, Hayley was discovering alternative, rock, and punk music. Bands like The Distillers, Green Day, and No Doubt piqued her interest. Hayley identified with these artists because they were rebellious and refused to fit neatly into a box.

It was the attitude as much as the song. Hayley identified with the rebellious attitude of the artists she adored, even at such a young age. She sometimes struggled to feel like she belonged in Meridian, but their music offered her that feeling. Hayley started experimenting with her voice and challenging herself to hit unpolished and raw notes as she became more involved in alternative music. Her voice began to take shape, becoming intense, passionate, and occasionally purposefully off-key. The foundation of her unique sound was created when the energy of punk rock combined with the emotional intensity she had absorbed from gospel music.

Hayley's passion for music was fostered at home but also increased friction. She started to sense the confines of her surroundings the more she threw herself into her musical goals. She was not content with the peaceful existence in a small town like Meridian could provide. She had visions of lights, stages, and a global audience for her songs. But that dream appeared far away, nearly unattainable. At the time, it felt like Meridian wasn't where future rock stars were made.

Everything changed when Hayley's family relocated to the Nashville suburb of Franklin, Tennessee. Hayley was about to start a new chapter in her life that would bring opportunities and challenges she had not yet realized as her childhood in Meridian ended with the relocation. Meridian was a world away from Nashville. Artists flocked to this city to leave their mark because of its rich musical history. Hayley saw a gain as well as a loss in the relocation. She was entering a world where her goals no longer seemed so distant, but she was also leaving behind the comfortable familiarity of her hometown.

Hayley was anxious and excited as the family packed their things and got ready to relocate. She knew moving away from Meridian meant bidding farewell to the security of her upbringing while welcoming the unknown and the opportunity to forge her course. She had no idea that this decision would usher in a new era in her life—one in which she would go from being a young woman from a tiny town with lofty aspirations to a worldwide rock star.

Meridian may have been the starting point of Hayley's narrative, but it was never intended to end there. Those latter things—the music, the hardships, and the victories—were paved over in those formative years. Hayley first experienced the beauty of vulnerability, the power of music, and the strength that comes from accepting oneself despite feeling like the world is too small in Meridian.

Moving to Nashville: Where Music Found Her

In Hayley Williams' life, relocating to Nashville was nothing short of a seismic transformation. The days of growing up in Meridian, Mississippi's little town, with its peaceful streets and well-known residents, were long gone. When Hayley was just 13 years old, she was thrown into a completely different environment where music was the lifeblood of the city rather than just a hobby or a passion. The family made their home in Franklin, Tennessee, a suburb of Nashville, the center of the American music industry. With this decision, Hayley would embark on a journey that would change her life—from a shy, aspiring singer to the lead singer of one of her generation's most recognizable alternative rock bands.

Hayley has never encountered anything like Nashville before. She sensed the electricity in the air the instant they arrived. The great musical legacy of the city could not be disregarded. Legends like Johnny Cash, Dolly Parton, and numerous others who started their careers from nothing and relied only on their ability and willpower called this place home. It was an exciting and terrifying environment for Hayley, where aspirations were built and dashed. Nashville was full of artists, singers, and composers fighting for their turn in the spotlight; she was no longer a small fish in a small pond.

Hayley didn't feel overwhelmed, though; instead, she felt alive. At last, she found a location where she could follow her passion for music, something she could never have done in Meridian.

Hayley didn't immediately start a profession when she moved to Nashville. Her parents' divorce, a challenging adjustment for the family, was the reason behind the transfer. But for Hayley, the promise of something fresh was mixed with the anguish of that breakup. With all of its resources, Nashville gave her a way to express the inner upheaval she was experiencing. She had always used music as an emotional release, and now she needed that outlet more than ever. Hayley started writing and singing renewedly in a city built on song, expressing the uncertainty, hopelessness, and bewilderment she was feeling throughout this significant life transformation.

While attending Franklin School, Hayley was surrounded by children who were passionate about music. This was a huge change compared to her life in Meridian, where she frequently felt alone or alienated from her peers. Here, music was a way of life rather than just a pastime. Nashville had a beat, and Hayley soon discovered that she was keeping time. She began attending writing workshops and taking voice lessons, devoting herself entirely to the creative process. People around her were drawn to her voice, which was developing beyond her years of age, and soon she was becoming well-known in the community.

Hayley's early years in Nashville were marked by several significant events, including her enrollment in a nearby school when she first made friends with Josh and Zac Farro. The three of them rapidly became close because of their mutual love of punk and alternative rock. The brothers were equally passionate about music. Hayley was drawn to punk's raw, intense passion, but many of her peers were more interested in country music—Nashville's bread and butter. She was greatly influenced by bands like Green Day and The Distillers because she connected with their music's rebellion and sincerity. Josh and Zac shared her passion for the genre, and the three began experimenting with their sound.

Combining the brothers' razor-sharp instruments with Hayley's powerful vocals, the three started creating and rehearsing in garages and basements. These early rehearsals were simple: just a handful of young people with a dream and a love of music. But there was something special about their relationship even in those modest beginnings. They became increasingly aware that they were on to something remarkable as they continued to play. Though none of them could have imagined the heights they would achieve at the time, the band that would eventually become Paramore was beginning to take shape.

Hayley found a new identity in Nashville, away from her budding musical career. She had frequently felt constrained in Meridian as if she didn't quite match the stereotype of a little child growing up in a typical Southern town. However, she started experimenting with her appearance, attitude, and style in Nashville. She adopted the punk look that complemented the music she adored, colored her hair vivid hues, and dressed provocatively and out of the ordinary. She could embrace the person she was becoming through this type of self-expression—someone who wasn't scared to stand out and go against the grain. For Hayley, Nashville represented more than simply a fresh start—it was a location where she could finally be authentic.

Hayley started collaborating with more seasoned Nashville producers and songwriters as her career as an artist developed. Thanks to her innate talent and unique voice, she stood out in a city where everyone seemed to pursue the same dream. Hayley was grateful for the chance to work with seasoned pros, but she never forgot why she fell in love with music in the first place. She aimed to produce something real related to her feelings and experiences. She had no interest in penning polished, radio-friendly pop tunes that are Nashville's standard. Instead, she was drawn to the honest, gritty storytelling of rock and punk, genres that allowed her to be unfiltered and open.

It was sometimes challenging to maintain this commitment to be authentic. Even though Nashville is a creative hub, it's possible that young artists there have been forced to conform to a particular style or vibe. Hayley was pressured to fit in and change her look to something more appealing to the masses. She resisted, though. She was unwilling to compromise and had a firm idea of what she wanted to achieve, even as a youngster. This inner fortitude would define her career as she battled to uphold her artistic integrity in a field that frequently put money before passion.

Hayley's relationship with the Farro brothers grew stronger over the months, and their casual jam sessions turned into more serious affairs. They started a band, and Paramore was formed after adding other local musicians. The band's early years were spent developing songs, rehearsing, and doing little shows throughout Nashville. Even though they were losing money and success looked unattainable, Hayley had always desired this life. Her identity as a musician was evolving beyond its first use as a means of expressing her feelings.

With its blend of creativity and history, Nashville provided the ideal setting for Paramore's ascent. The city recognized the value of hard effort, storytelling, and honesty. Even though Paramore's sound was very different from Nashville's traditional country style, fans were nevertheless struck by the band's intense live shows and unadulterated passion. They gained popularity gradually but steadily for their music and Hayley's captivating onstage persona. Her magnetic quality pulled people in even at a young age; her strength and fragility combined made her impossible to ignore.

Hayley's relationship with Nashville got stronger as Paramore's local success increased. The city has become her home because of its extensive musical history. There, she discovered her mission, her band, and her voice. It had been a leap of faith to relocate to Nashville and a voyage into the unknown. However, that's when Hayley found her calling. Nashville was more than simply the town she called home; it was also where she discovered herself and music.

CHAPTER 2: FINDING PARAMORE

The Birth of Paramore: A New Band on the Scene

Hayley Williams' journey from an aspiring vocalist to the lead singer of Paramore was not only the product of skill but also a perfect storm of opportunity, teamwork, and an unwavering love for music. The formation of Paramore signaled a turning point in the alternative rock scene by bringing a new sound and energy that would appeal to fans everywhere. As Hayley and her bandmates started to carve out their place in the music industry, they overcame many obstacles. They achieved many victories that helped to define their personalities and bring them to the forefront.

Following Hayley's move to Nashville, where she met brothers Josh and Zac Farro, Paramore was formed. Their passion for punk and alternative rock, particularly, brought them together. They had what it took to be remarkable, from Hayley's potent voice and the brothers' skill in the instruments. What started as informal jam sessions in basements and garages quickly developed into a dedication to making original music—an endeavor defining their adolescence and beyond.

As they started penning songs together, Hayley quickly became a prolific lyricist. She had an unrivaled capacity to convey the nuances of adolescent turmoil, loss, and resilience. The song's intensely personal yet broadly relevant lyrics perfectly captured the highs and lows of puberty. With a blend of infectious tunes and accurate insights into the difficulties of maturing, songs like "Pressure" and "Conspiracy" captured the frustrations of adolescence. This distinctive fusion of catchy tunes and meaningful words became a defining characteristic of Paramore's music.

The band's early years were characterized by a will to leave their imprint despite challenges. They had to deal with the same challenges that any new band faces: developing a sound, getting gigs, and gaining fans. Hayley's ambition was so strong that she frequently took the lead in band promotion, using social media and local music scenes to get the word out. Often armed only with a demo tape and a goal, she persistently pursued opportunities to perform by reaching out to local venues.

The band started performing at local festivals and bars as they developed their craft, earning a reputation for their exciting shows. Their live performance was electrifying, drawing spectators in with a blend of the Farro brothers' guitar riffs and Hayley's powerful vocals. They attracted new admirers with every show, captivated by Hayley's captivating charisma as much as their sound. Even in more extensive settings, she had a unique capacity to connect with her audience and make every concert feel powerful and intimate.

The moment Paramore was founded by a local management team who realized their potential and the chance to assist them in reaching a larger audience was a turning point in their career. Through this relationship, doors that had previously appeared unattainable were unlocked. The band was keen to capture the raw energy of their live performances and was able to enter the studio for the first time with the help of resources and instruction. The process of recording was thrilling as well as intimidating. They would be in a professional environment now, but they would be true to who they were.

2005 saw the release of Paramore's first album, "All We Know Is Falling." The band's early hardships and the emotional impact of their songs were captured in the title alone. It blended pop-punk intensity and heartfelt vocals, a genuine and honest portrayal of their experiences. Hits like "Pressure" and "Emergency" showed off the band's ability to combine appealing melodies with a punk edge and highlighted Hayley's vocal range and lyrical profundity. Listeners found a connection with the record, especially those going through a turbulent adolescence.

As "All We Know Is Falling" started to gain momentum, big record labels began to take notice. Paramore's songs' melodic blend of emotional transparency and teenage defiance resonated with a generation weary of polished pop and yearned for authenticity. The band's fan base was increasing, and they were thirsty for more, so they soon went from local favorites to national competitors.

Their first album's success opened doors for them to perform with well-known bands, which increased their popularity and impact even further. They started touring and sharing stages with groups like My Chemical Romance and Fall Out Boy, giving them exposure and vital experience. Every performance served as a platform for showcasing their music, and Hayley's popularity grew as she accepted her role as the frontwoman.

But strain also accompanied success. The group had to navigate the music business while staying loyal to their origins. As anticipation increased and they got ready to record their second album, they struggled to balance artistic growth with maintaining Paramore's core identity. Despite the pressure to live up to the expectations placed on her as the band's face, Hayley was adamant about keeping the genuineness that had carried the group this far.

With the release of "Riot!," their breakthrough album that would propel them into the mainstream and cement their place in rock history, Paramore made history in 2007. With singles like "That's What You Get," "Misery Business," and "Crushcrushcrush," the album displayed a sophisticated sound that struck a mix between pop sensibility and rock ferocity. Every song featured Hayley's incredible voice, and her lyrical tales struck a chord with admirers who took comfort in her words.

The movie "Riot!" had a significant effect. The album launched Paramore into new heights of financial success and garnering critical praise. Their committed fan base always anticipated their every move, and they became a regular feature on music charts and radio stations. Although the band's success was rapid, Hayley stayed grounded. She was resolved to move forward authentically because she realized that the road was just as essential as the destination.

Hayley Williams became a symbol of empowerment and resiliency through the ups and downs of founding Paramore. The band's narrative was one of cooperation, tenacity, and persistent faith in the transformative power of music. In a congested music scene, Paramore stood out thanks to their distinctive sound and Hayley's captivating presence. This allowed them to leave a legacy inspiring numerous musicians for years.

Paramore never lost sight of their origins even as they developed further. Hayley's transformation from a little Meridian girl to the lead singer of a well-known rock group proves the strength of ambition, willpower, and enduring friendship. The formation of Paramore was more than just the formation of a band; it was the result of Hayley's constant love of music and her desire to use her art to communicate with people. Even though the voyage was starting, it was already apparent that Paramore would have a lasting impact on the music industry.

The First Breakthrough

Within the turbulent atmosphere of teenage life and the fast-paced music industry in Nashville, the publication of Paramore's first album, "All We Know Is Falling," was a turning point for the band and Hayley Williams' career as a rising musician. This record spoke to a generation struggling with its intricacies because it captured a genuine, visceral honesty. It was the first accurate indication of the band's talent and an introspective trip through confusion, heartbreak, and the bittersweet aches of growing up.

Hayley decided to record "All We Know Is Falling" at a crucial juncture in her life. Her music was influenced by her experience negotiating the turmoil of her parents' divorce at the tender age of sixteen. This internal strife created the album's deep emotional background. Her longing and grief were transformed into solid and moving melodies in each song, which acted as a cathartic release. The lyrics have a strong emotional impact, reflecting her challenges and the everyday experiences of adolescence, heartbreak, and self-discovery.

The process of recording the CD was both thrilling and intimidating. Driven to preserve their distinct sound while capturing the unadulterated energy of their live performances, the band approached the studio with a sense of urgency. Hayley put much effort and love into every song, as did the Farro brothers and their bandmates. They knew this album was more than just a selection of songs; it served as a platform to introduce themselves to the public and set the stage for a successful career launch or an eventual decline into obscurity.

"All We Know Is Falling" was produced by veteran producer David Bendeth, who has worked with several rock acts. He oversaw Paramore's sonic experimentation, combining pop-punk elements with melodic, reflective tones. Hayley's voice, which combines power and delicacy, emerged as the album's main attraction. Her voice was unparalleled in its ability to emote vulnerability, and this emotional sincerity distinguished Paramore from its peers.

The band included songs representing their experiences as up-and-coming musicians attempting to find their way in the music business as the tracks developed. "All We Know," the album's lead single, set the mood with its eerie sounds and reflective lyrics. Those who felt lost may relate to the themes of loss and longing. Hayley's varied vocal range and emotional depth were emphasized by the song's contrast of quiet verses and strong choruses, which drew listeners in and encouraged them to identify with her experience.

"Pressure," the second tune on the album, demonstrated the band's upbeat tone even further. It encapsulated the tension that comes with expectations, both internal and external, as well as the need to overcome their burden. With its intense guitar tones and powerful vocals by Hayley, "Pressure" immediately won over listeners. The song's unadulterated energy reflected the band's youthful enthusiasm and will to forge their way in a field that frequently attempted to categorize musicians into particular genres.

With the composition of "All We Know Is Falling," Hayley became increasingly engrossed in the songwriting process. She tapped into her generation's everyday experiences to write incredibly personal and approachable lyrics. One of the album's best songs, "Emergency," explored themes of urgency and the need to make decisions when facing emotional turmoil. The band and their fans felt a sense of solidarity due to the song's resonance with people feeling similarly overtaken by their circumstances.

The album's lyrical tone expressed hope and reflected Hayley's problems. A message beneath all of the chaos spoke to fortitude and the strength of progress. This feeling was aptly captured in the last song, "My Heart," which had sentimental lyrics that expressed a need for understanding and connection. The album came to a strong close, giving listeners a sense of emotional closure.

The July 2005 release of "All We Know Is Falling" signaled the start of a new chapter in Paramore's history. Numerous critics praised the album's unique emotional depth and youthful energy blend. It wasn't a commercial success, but it made waves in the alternative music community and set the stage for future success. The band's dedication to their sound and Hayley's genuineness drew in fans, building a devoted fan base that would only increase over time.

Due to the album's early success, Paramore started touring and introducing more people to their music by playing at festivals and local venues. These early gigs essentially established their live reputation. Hayley gained recognition for her ability to interact with the audience and create a cozy ambiance even in larger spaces because of her captivating stage presence. Every performance served as a chance to establish a more personal connection with the audience and increase the band's standing in their eyes.

After "All We Know Is Falling" was released, touring was an exciting and challenging experience. The band, still in its early stages as musicians, had to contend with the hardships of touring while adjusting to their newly adult duties. Their determination was tested by the demands of performing night after night and the individual struggles they were all going through. Nevertheless, Hayley's drive and leadership kept the group concentrated on their common objectives.

Following the album's release, record labels and industry insiders started to take an interest in Paramore. Thanks to their distinctive sound and captivating onstage persona, they became highly sought-after in the rapidly changing alternative music scene. Their rise in popularity translated into more possibilities for them, resulting in turning points that determined their course in the music business.

In the end, "All We Know Is Falling" provided a vital basis for Paramore's success in the future. The record perfectly captured both the complexity of emotional experiences and the rawness of youth. It enabled Hayley Williams and her bandmates to speak their truths and welcome listeners into their world with its moving lyrics and catchy tunes. This debut album had a profound effect beyond its initial release; it helped Paramore develop into a band that would connect with millions of listeners and encourage others to find their voice through music.

Looking back, "All We Know Is Falling" was more than simply an album; it was a sincere proclamation of resilience, identity, and the ability of music to unite people from all walks of life. For Hayley, it was the start of a career that would see her develop from a dream-chasing youngster to a critical figure in the rock music industry. The record served as a monument to the setbacks, victories, and steadfast spirit that would define her career and shape her work for many years.

CHAPTER 3: FAME AND FRACTURES

"Riot!" and Stardom: Paramore's Meteoric Rise

The unstoppable Hayley Williams and other members' skills, strategic choices, and creative innovation all contributed to the group's incredible ascent. After their debut album was released, Paramore experienced a lot of transformation. They had accumulated countless hours of touring, honing their sound and stage presence and building a loyal following. Their musical orientation was molded by the lessons they acquired from touring. Hayley started participating more actively in songwriting since she felt more comfortable in her role as frontwoman. Her lyrics became increasingly passionate, expressing a wide range of issues that spoke to the youth of the day in addition to her own experiences.

David Bendeth, who had previously collaborated on their debut album, produced "Riot!". Through this cooperation, the band could display a more refined sound while maintaining its raw intensity, as they could tap into their collective experiences. Pop-punk and alternative rock elements were combined to create an album distinguished by memorable melodies, energetic choruses, and Hayley's strong vocals, defining the band's sound.

The lead track, "Misery Business," debuted on the radio and instantly grabbed listeners' attention with its catchy energy and relatable lyrics. With its themes of rebellion and empowerment, the song served as a proclamation of independence. The band's upbeat instrumentation and Hayley's sassy delivery connected with a generation of young people ready to rebel against conventional norms. Paramore had a sea change due to its success; "Misery Business" rose to the top of the charts and won the band's praise from critics.

The popularity of "Riot!" caused Paramore's fan base to explode. A testament to the album's broad appeal, it went platinum after debuting at number 20 on the Billboard 200. At a time when social media was starting to change the music business, Paramore was skillfully using sites like MySpace to interact with their fan base. With updates on new music, behind-the-scenes tour photos, and personal anecdotes, Hayley and her bandmates actively interacted with their fanbase. Many fans developed a personal tie with the band due to this connection, which encouraged a sense of community and loyalty.

By adding themselves to the Warped Tour roster, they could perform live and establish themselves as a band that people had to see. Concertgoers were enthralled with Hayley's captivating stage presence because of her genuine charm and charisma. Regardless of the size of the stadium, she had a rare capacity to connect with her audience, making every concert feel personal and meaningful.

Songs like "That's What You Get," "Crushcrushcrush," and "When It Rains" demonstrated how songwriters have matured. The complexity of relationships, identity, and the difficulties of young adulthood were all reflected in Hayley's songs, which were laced with a mixture of strength and fragility. Every song had a narrative and offered anthems for empowerment while encouraging listeners to consider their own experiences.

The "Misery Business" music video cemented Paramore's position in popular culture even more. Its colorful graphics and intense performances perfectly encapsulated the band's rebellious and carefree spirit. Millions of people saw the video when it went viral, considerably boosting the band's rising fame. Their reach beyond the alternative scene was further expanded as it became a mainstay on music television networks.

Paramore was catapulted into stardom with the release of "Riot!" They received numerous honors and accolades, including a Grammy Award for Best New Artist. Although this recognition rewarded their diligence and hard work, it also presented new difficulties. The band was under a lot of pressure to build on their success, especially Hayley, the face and frontwoman of Paramore. It wasn't easy to juggle the obligations of recording, touring, and keeping up personal relationships.

Hayley stayed grounded despite the difficulties, crediting her bandmates' and fans' steadfast support for their triumph. She frequently discussed the value of authenticity in their music and the necessity of remaining loyal to oneself in the face of industry demands. This dedication moved fans to authenticity and valued the openness of Hayley's songs and the band's background.

The album set the standard for subsequent releases. Therefore, its legacy only grew from there. A new generation of musicians was inspired by "Riot!"'s inventiveness and enthusiasm, as well as by Hayley's unique vocals and the band's ability to merge genres effortlessly. In the face of hardship, Paramore represented fortitude and inventiveness, proving that success could be attained without sacrificing one's uniqueness.

Thanks to the whirlwind of celebrity, Harley grew and learned about herself while negotiating the challenges of being a young artist in the public eye. Her perception of her job as an artist and a voice for her generation has evolved due to each performance and interview.

Looking back, "Riot!" was more than just an album—it was a phenomenon that shaped a generation. With Hayley Williams leading the charge and promoting themes of honesty and empowerment, it perfectly captured the essence of adolescent rebellion and emotional exploration. The record had a far-reaching influence on the music industry and the lives of many followers beyond its financial success.

The knowledge gained during the "Riot!" era would form the basis for Paramore's upcoming projects, encouraging them to pursue novel artistic avenues while adhering to their core values. Fueled by "Riot!"'s popularity, Hayley's adventure was only getting started, and everyone was excited to see where her voice would lead her next. During this period, Paramore's rapid ascent to fame was evidence of the ability of music to foster self-expression, connection, and resiliency. It also permanently changed their careers and the lives of those they influenced.

Struggles Behind the Scenes: The Fracturing of the Band

The demands of the music business, combined with individual hardships, created a complicated web of connections that put the hitherto unshakable ties of friendship and teamwork to the test. Hayley Williams experienced a great deal of emotional hardship during this time as she dealt with her band's breakup and rising celebrity.

It was startling to shift from the thrill of quick achievement to the harsh reality of constant pressures. Following "Riot!" The band was thrown into an unbreakable cycle of recording, touring, and media appearances, with little time to reflect on their experiences. All of the band members suffered from the demands of frequent travel and media attention, but these factors heightened Hayley's emotions of loneliness. Although she was praised for being the face of Paramore, her public image concealed the inner challenges she went through as a young lady in the spotlight and a leader guiding a group through difficult times.

The Farro brothers, Josh and Zac, voiced their displeasure with the band's direction. The demands made of them and the artistic choices made, especially by Hayley and the band's management, made them feel more and more limited. The demanding nature of the music industry compounded this tension, resulting in disagreements over personal priorities and creative direction. As the band's creative director and spokesman,

Hayley had taken on a more forceful position and was now at odds with her longtime pals. She felt burdened with the need to uphold the band's success while staying true to their shared vision.

Paramore's members' individual lifestyles added to the band's emotional terrain. Hayley was battling both the demands of public life and her fears. She felt compelled to help her bandmates even though their relationships were strained as she worked to develop personally and artistically. Unspoken grievances and unresolved emotions now eclipsed the everyday experiences of touring, making songs, and growing up together. What had once been a place of happiness and friendship turned into a battlefield where everyone was battling their fears and goals.

Despite everything around her, Hayley tried to be honest with her bandmates. She thought transparency was essential to solve the fundamental problems endangering their unity. However, these conversations frequently became heated disputes that exposed underlying resentment and divergent ideas about Paramore's future. There was a lot of pressure to continue their commercial success, and each member had a unique outlook on handling the next stage of their careers.

"Brand New Eyes", the band's third studio album, captured the turbulent feelings they were going through and was released in 2010. Drawing from her experiences with grief, uncertainty, and the nuances of friendship, Hayley poured her heart and soul into the lyrics. Fans found great resonance in the album's themes of introspection and resilience, which also reflected the band's internal challenges. Songs like "Ignorance" and "The Only Exception" expressed the contradiction between the singers' inner prosperity and the image of success they presented to the outside world.

Despite receiving positive reviews and doing well at the box office, "Brand New Eyes" exposed the divisions within Paramore. The band's inability to maintain a unified face during the album's promotion was the source of the friction. As she became more conscious of the growing divide between her and her other band members' visions for the group, Hayley felt caught between the urge to embrace her artistic identity and the group's heritage.

When the Farro brothers announced their resignation from the band in late 2010, it was clear that these struggles had come to a head. Fans and business experts in the Paramore scene were left stunned by their departure. The band, which had felt unbeatable at one point, had a deeper fissure within; the split represented more than just the departure of two important members. Hayley was inconsolable, lamenting not just the passing of her bandmates but also the breakup of the relationships and collaborations she had loved for such a long time.

Following the breakup, Hayley experienced a severe emotional breakdown. She felt pressure to keep going as Paramore and was even more terrified of losing everything they had fought for. As the band's primary spokesperson, she was thrown into the position of assuring fans and fielding the inevitable inquiries concerning Paramore's future. The loss of her lifelong friends saddened her, but she also felt obligated to uphold the legacy they had created.

Hayley was forced to face her own identity as an artist during this turbulent time. She struggled with the expectations put on her and the contradiction of being a leader and a collaborator. The Farro brothers' departure forced her, in many respects, to reevaluate her goals for Paramore and to give herself more creative freedom. It was a challenging but essential transition that would help her better grasp her voice and goals as an artist.

Hayley was open and honest about her difficulties and the value of honesty in her music in interviews that followed the breakup. Reflecting on the lessons discovered throughout those turbulent years, she emphasized the importance of candid communication and being prepared to face complex realities. Even while it was a painful experience, it also pushed her to accept her uniqueness and learn how to manage the challenges of being a band leader, which aided in her personal development.

The tale of Paramore during this period demonstrates the difficulties many musicians encounter in striking a balance between their personal and professional goals. Hayley's experience navigating the band's breakup shed light on the reality of celebrity, friendship, and the creative process. Behind-the-scenes challenges weren't just roadblocks; they were crucial times that influenced Hayley Williams' career as an artist and the direction Paramore would take.

Hayley emerged from the chaos with a fresh sense of resolve and purpose. Although the voyage had been burdensome, it had also been life-changing. It allowed her to reinvent what Paramore may become and opened the door to a new world of possibilities. Through the hardships, she discovered the importance of authenticity and resilience in the face of misfortune; this lesson would reverberate in her music for years to come.

CHAPTER 4: THE WOMAN BEHIND THE MICROPHONE

Mental Health Battles: Anxiety and Depression

Along with her artistic achievements, Hayley Williams's rise to popularity has been accompanied by significant psychological challenges, most notably anxiety and depression. Her life has been profoundly impacted by these mental health struggles, which are frequently hidden and stigmatized. They have affected her sense of self and her artistic vision. Her mental health started to suffer as she dealt with the difficulties of celebrity, including the strain of public life and the weight of expectations.

After "Riot!" came out, Hayley had a brief period of popularity, which is when her anxiousness first appeared.

An exhausting schedule of nonstop media appearances, touring, and unrelenting fan and reviewer scrutiny accompanied gained notoriety. Hayley had to deal with the realities of living in a fishbowl even as her career took off. The unrelenting attention heightened her fears, and she started having panic attacks and intense periods of self-doubt. This was a far cry from her carefree childhood when creating music seemed like an unadulterated creative expression rather than a stressful endeavor.

Hayley's relationship problems and the personal difficulties she had in the band made her anxiousness worse. She frequently felt alone as the strain increased and found it difficult to express her emotions to those around her. Her conflicts became more intense due to the expectations put on her as the face of Paramore, which trapped her in a vicious cycle of self-criticism and overanalyzing. Maintaining a pristine façade while dealing with mental health issues became a taxing facade that was challenging to keep up.

Despite her growing notoriety, Hayley was committed to being true to herself. She broke the taboo around mental health concerns in the music industry by being candid about them in interviews. She was pretty open about her anxiety and despair, highlighting the fact that vulnerability is a strength rather than a weakness. Hayley hoped that by talking about her experiences, she would normalize the discourse about mental health and encourage others to get support. She wanted to create a space where her admirers felt understood, knowing that many were probably going through similar things.

It became more and more clear how her mental health affected the songs she wrote. Hayley used her music to express her feelings, pouring her troubles into her lyrics. Songs like "Anklebiters" and "Hate to See Your Heart Break," from the album "Paramore" highlight her inner struggles and the difficulties of overcoming obstacles in life. Fans connected with these songs because they captured the heartbreak and worry that frequently accompanies personal development. Hayley found comfort and a sense of purpose by directing her suffering into her work, which helped her connect with listeners who recognized themselves in her lyrics.

Hayley sought therapy as part of her healing journey because she knew that getting help from a professional was essential to maintaining her mental health. Through treatment, she was able to manage her anxiety and address the underlying problems that were causing her misery. This self-discovery journey allowed her to explore her emotions more deeply and gain a deeper understanding of herself as a person and an artist of self-discovery. She developed greater empathy and self-awareness as she dealt with her mental health issues, both on and off stage.

Even yet, Hayley encountered obstacles in her path. Anxiety can be a fickle foe, and periods of uncertainty can come back with ease, especially when things are stressful. Once thrilling, public appearances and performances now cause anxiety and have the potential to cause panic attacks. She forced herself to resist giving in to these emotions while performing by reminding herself of the happiness that music gave her. She relied on her bandmates' and her fans' support during those times, finding strength in the community that had come together to support her.

The music business has had a broader debate about mental health because of Hayley's openness about her issues. She has motivated many of her fans to prioritize their mental health and get treatment when necessary by candidly sharing her struggles. Because of her openness, her audience has grown more supportive of one another, forming a community where people don't feel as alone in their challenges. Hayley's willingness to accept vulnerability has provided a welcome viewpoint in a society that frequently exalts perfection, emphasizing the value of self-acceptance and honesty.

Following her difficulties, Hayley has also shifted her attention to activism. She has collaborated with numerous mental health groups and used her influence to spread the word about the value of mental health resources. Her endeavors to spread the word that it's acceptable not to feel okay have included speaking appearances, social media initiatives, and partnerships with mental health specialists. Hayley wants to eliminate the stigma associated with mental health problems and inspire people to put their health first by using her influence.

For Hayley, controlling her anxiety and sadness is a continuous process that requires daily self-care and self-compassion. She now understands that the healing process is a sequence of ups and downs, victories and setbacks. With this knowledge, she has developed resilience and accepted that failures do not make her less talented or valuable.

The difficulties Hayley Williams has had with her mental health serve as a moving reminder of the complexity of both celebrity and the human condition. She has changed many people's lives and changed her own by being vulnerable and encouraging an atmosphere of support and openness. Her tale is one of bravery, sincerity, and tenacity—a monument to the strength of accepting one's difficulties and turning them into an opportunity for personal development. Hayley continues to be a ray of hope for people going through similar struggles, letting them know they're not traveling alone as she navigates the complexities of life and art.

Redefining Identity: Who is Hayley Williams?

Hayley Williams underwent a deep voyage of self-discovery as she navigated the complex terrain of celebrity and personal development. This trip forced her to face who she was outside her role as Paramore's lead vocalist. She had to redefine who she was in the face of both public and private hardships, and this process became a significant part of her story. It was about more than simply her musical ability; it was about realizing her depths, her goals, the core of her being.

Hayley had always been creative from her early years in Meridian, Mississippi, but the magnitude of her celebrity changed her in ways she could not have predicted. Expectations grew as she evolved from a teenage girl hoping to become a famous musician to a world-renowned figure. Her personal life started to blend in with the image of the energetic, self-assured frontwoman that her fans loved. She was forced to seek clarity and authenticity due to the intense internal battle resulting from the clash between her public image and inner reality.

Hayley frequently found herself stuck in a box that other people's opinions had created during the hectic period of her ascent to prominence. It became more challenging for her to reconcile these different personas with her personality as fans, critics, and the media all had other ideas about who she was. She frequently felt inadequate due to the pressure to uphold a specific image, making people wonder if she was good outside of music. And when the spotlight went down, who was Hayley Williams? When the cheers died down, who was she?

As she confronted the truth of her mental health issues, her contemplation grew deeper. For Hayley, anxiety and despair served as triggers for more in-depth thought since they are frequent battles waged in silence. Through counseling and self-discovery, she removed the characteristics that made her who she was. She tried to discover her true priorities beyond titles, awards, and fame. This quest was about more than just conquering hardship; it was about taking back her story and rediscovering her essential principles.

Hayley understood the value of honesty in her personal and artistic endeavors as she struggled with her identity. This insight proved to be a game-changer for her, as she began to see vulnerability as a strength rather than a weakness. She became increasingly aware that her genuine strength came from her willingness to be open and sincere the more she opened up about her experiences, setbacks, and victories. By doing this, she not only freed herself but also gave her narrative inspiration to a significant number of admirers.

Music evolved into a crucial medium for this self-exploration process. With time, Hayley's songs became an intensely personal journal that expressed her dreams, concerns, and experiences. She imbued her songs with open examinations of identity, self-acceptance, and the intricacies of relationships with albums like "Paramore" and "After Laughter". Every song represented her shifting emotional terrain and mental state, acting as a stepping stone in her journey to a deeper understanding of herself. Songs like "Hard Times" captured the challenges of managing mental health, and "Told You So" spoke to taking control of one's story in the face of hardship.

Hayley started questioning conventional expectations of femininity and strength as part of her journey to rethink her identity. She experienced additional pressure to live up to stereotypes of what a female artist should sound, look, and behave like because she was a woman working in the male-dominated music industry. But Hayley fought against these limitations. She developed a distinct sense of style and presence by embracing her originality. By doing this, she inspired other women to reject the constraints of societal norms and embrace their unique personalities fearlessly.

Hayley's aim to promote community and connection was also mirrored in this identity progression. She learned more and more about the value of providing a haven for others as she went along. She aimed to promote discussions about mental health, self-acceptance, and authenticity through her speeches, music, and social media. She gave her supporters the confidence to embrace their travels by being honest about her vulnerabilities and reassuring them that they were not alone in their problems.

Hayley's development brought her closer to her ideals and interests outside of music. She investigated her passions for activism, art, and fashion and realized how vital these areas were to who she was. Her sense of self was further enhanced by her ability to express different aspects of herself through her work with other designers and her commitment to social causes. With each undertaking, her identity was better understood, supporting the notion that identity is a dynamic combination of experiences, interests, and beliefs rather than a fixed set of characteristics.

In the end, reinventing her identity led to a profound realization that Hayley Williams is a complex person who is a friend, singer, activist, and always-changing person. This insight freed her from the limitations of what the general public thought of her, enabling her to accept her complexity proudly. She learned that it was acceptable to be a work in progress, not to have all the answers, and to enjoy life's convoluted yet exquisite adventure.

This identity search has affected her relationship with Paramore in the larger scheme of her career. She learned how to balance appreciating her bandmates' talents and standing up for herself as she negotiated the changing relationships within the group. This harmony became essential in determining Paramore's future since it permitted development and evolution without losing sight of their shared past. The band's discussions about identity reflected Hayley's journey and created a space for each member to express their uniqueness while pursuing a common objective.

CHAPTER 5: STEPPING INTO THE SPOTLIGHT

Solo Artist: The Journey to "Petals for Armor"

When Hayley Williams started her solo career, she traveled through unfamiliar territory on a personal and musical level. Her move from frontwoman of Paramore to solo artist involved a deeper investigation of her identity, inventiveness, and grit than just a change in artistic direction. Her road toward "Petals for Armor", her debut solo album, was a crucial phase in her life, a rich tapestry of self-discovery, exploration, and contemplation.

The seeds of her solo endeavor were planted against the turbulent backdrop of her mental health issues and the changing dynamics of Paramore. Hayley felt compelled to express her uniqueness after years of dedicating herself to the band, creating a place where she could experiment with various sounds and ideas that spoke to her experiences. Her desire to connect with her inner self inspired her when she started writing the music that would become "Petals for Armor."

Following her bandmates' exit and emotional upheaval, Hayley turned to songwriting to process her feelings. Writing gave her the courage to face her hopes, anxieties, and vulnerabilities. Every song became an exposed fragment of her soul, a direct and honest way for her to absorb her feelings and experiences. This openness allowed her to go further into contemplative subjects and examine the nuances of her mental health difficulties, which was a break from the frequently high-energy, joyful style of Paramore's music.

"Petals for Armor" was developed through experimentation as well. Hayley seized the chance to work with various artists and producers, expanding the possibilities for her voice. She was allowed to experiment with multiple musical genres, including pop, alternative rock, folk, and even R&B, which reflected her wish to defy the expectations placed on her band. She developed new aspects of her craft with every partnership, which let her broaden her sound pallet without sacrificing her essential character.

Hayley took inspiration for her songs from a variety of experiences in her life, such as her struggles with depression and anxiety, her relationships with others, and her search for self-acceptance. Her songs, which addressed empowerment, healing, and loss, were remarkably vulnerable. Songs like "Simmer" and "Leave It Alone" demonstrated her ability to express complicated feelings in a heartfelt and honest manner, striking a chord with audiences who took comfort in her lyrics. Hayley became a storyteller and a singer over this lyrical journey, crafting tales that reflected her setbacks and victories.

Reclaiming her story was one of the most transforming components of her solo project. Hayley felt free after she broke free from the restrictions of being known only as Paramore's frontwoman. She accepted that she could be more than just a musician and that she could also be an artist, an activist, and a woman who freely explores her identity. Her newfound independence gave her the confidence to question conventional notions of femininity and strength and what it means to be a woman in the music business.

Hayley put her mental health first when she was creating "Petals for Armor." She learned the value of self-care and mindfulness from her past experiences and the demands of the music business. She tried establishing a space free from worry and judgment-averse dread to encourage creativity. As she investigated the relationship between creativity and emotional well-being, her emphasis on mental health became increasingly central to the album's story.

Hayley's will to be in charge of her story was further demonstrated by her choice to release "Petals for Armor" as a trilogy of EPs. She was able to delve further into various ideas and feelings with each EP—"Petals for Armor: Volume 1," "Volume 2," and "Volume 3"—resulting in a more complex portrayal of her journey. This strategy emphasized that identity is a multidimensional experience rather than a linear one, mirroring her progress. Fans were captivated by the suspense surrounding each release, allowing Hayley to update her tale as it happened.

When the first volume was released in 2020, critics well-received it. It demonstrated Hayley's development as an artist and her capacity for building strong connections with her audience. Fans responded to the frank honesty of songs like "Over Yet" and "Cinnamon" because they encapsulated the courage and tenderness that had come to define her path. The album's tone was new and familiar, and it had a blend of inspirations that demonstrated her artistic development and retained the emotional depth that had always defined her work.

Hayley Williams established herself as a formidable solo performer by publishing "Petals for Armor." She created a place for herself that was different from Paramore but still very much a part of her heritage. The album cemented her status as a unique artist, highlighting her adaptability and daring nature—attributes that won over new and old admirers alike.

There were difficulties on the way to "Petals for Armor." Hayley experienced periods of self-doubt, wondering if she could emerge from Paramore's shadow and succeed as a solo performer. But each obstacle served as a springboard for her development, encouraging her to embrace her distinct voice and narrative. Ultimately, she succeeded not just as a musician but also as a representation of fortitude and genuineness.

Healing Through Music: Vulnerability in Her Lyrics

Hayley Williams has been praised for her ability to engage listeners with incredibly intimate and frequently sensitive lyrics for a considerable amount of time. Her songwriting is more than just entertainment; it's a way for her and her listeners to find catharsis. This relationship highlights the therapeutic potential of music as a medium, enabling the expression and understanding of emotions in ways spoken words frequently fail to do.

Hayley has been reflecting on her inner turmoil and personal situations through her lyrics since the early days of her Paramore career. Her songs are filled with themes of love, heartache, and self-discovery, which resonate with listeners who recognize themselves reflected in her words. Every song serves as a medium for shared experiences, giving listeners a secure and understanding environment to work with their emotions. In addition to fostering a sense of connection, this authenticity builds a community of people connected by their common vulnerabilities.

Hayley's lyrics from her early albums, especially "All We Know Is Falling". Songs like "Pressure" and "Misery Business" encapsulated the turbulent feelings of adolescence, including bewilderment, annoyance, and a desire for acceptance. Hayley gave her audience a voice and a platform to tackle their fears by being open and honest about these emotions. These songs' anthemic quality make them rallying cries for people facing comparable problems in addition to making them catchy. Singing along turned into a group healing process where people could let go of bottled-up feelings and find comfort in one another.

Hayley's songwriting developed along with her artistic and psychological growth. The albums "Paramore" and "After Laughter" showed the shift to more reflective topics. She addressed the complexity of mental health, despair, and the mask frequently worn in public life in songs like "Fake Happy" and "Hard Times." These lyrics, honest about the layers of pressure and expectations she endured as a public figure, reveal much about her troubles. By sharing her inner struggles, Hayley encourages her audience to consider their own experiences with mental health and promotes conversation on frequently stigmatized subjects.

For Hayley and her supporters, communicating these hardships via song is a healing process. For example, in "Fake Happy," the contrast between cheerful instrumentals and depressing lyrics effectively captures the paradox of seeming happy but struggling with inner pain. Many people under pressure to keep up a front may relate to this complexity, which frees them up to face their feelings head-on. In a world where she can sometimes feel alone, Hayley's ability to so beautifully express these emotions gives listeners a safe environment to examine their vulnerabilities and fosters a sense of belonging.

With the release of her solo album "Petals for Armor," Hayley's lyrical vulnerability underwent a dramatic transformation. This project shows her profound discovery of self-healing, and artistic development. The songs explore complex issues of identity, love, and empowerment. Songs like "Simmer" and "Leave It Alone" demonstrate her courage to face life's messiness head-on and her ability to articulate the complexity of human emotion with grace and honesty. She portrays the simmering conflicts that can occur in relationships in "Simmer," and in "Leave It Alone," she considers the value of admitting suffering rather than trying to hide it. The song's lyrics serve as a universal story and a personal journal, giving listeners comfort in knowing they are not alone in their experiences with loss and resiliency.

Moreover, Hayley's public demeanor is infused with a tenderness transcending her poetic substance. She has developed into a mental health advocate, frequently sharing on social media and in interviews about her struggles with depression and anxiety. This transparency helps to de-stigmatize mental health concerns in the music industry and beyond, in addition to supporting the themes in her songs. She encourages her followers to ask for assistance and support by normalizing talks about these subjects, fostering a compassionate and understanding community.

Hayley's dedication to genuineness highlights the tension between vulnerability and healing in her music. She has discussed the importance of being authentic and accepting one's flaws. Her songs, where she accepts her imperfections and uncertainties rather than ignoring them, are infused with this concept. By doing this, Hayley connects with listeners who struggle with accepting who they are while also humanizing herself. Her openness encourages followers to take their frailties and creates a space where mutual understanding can lead to healing.

CHAPTER 6: CREATIVITY IN COLOR

Beyond Music: Fashion and Good Dye Young

Hayley Williams is a versatile artist whose influence extends beyond the music industry. She has always been more than just a musical legend. Her entry into the fashion and beauty industries, especially with her hair color line Good Dye Young, demonstrates her dedication to individuality and creativity in all its forms. Her foray into the fashion and cosmetics industries reflects her sense of style and her goal of encouraging others to value their uniqueness.

Since her early days as Paramore's frontwoman, Hayley has drawn notice from the media and fans for her daring wardrobe choices. She has continuously pushed boundaries, reinventing what it means to be a rock star in the modern music scene with her vivid hair colors, unique costumes, and bold makeup. Her aesthetic, which embodies themes of sincerity, resistance, and empowerment, frequently reflects the emotional depth of her songs. Hayley sends a strong message with her appearance: uniqueness should be embraced rather than repressed.

By introducing Good Dye Young, a hair color brand that prioritizes vibrant colors and artistic expression, in 2016, Hayley made a big step toward expressing her creativity outside of music. Her experiences with hair coloring, a habit she has followed her entire life, gave rise to the brand. She has been able to explore her identity through hair color, showcasing various aspects of her personality. She wanted to give her followers and customers the means to use hair color to express their creativity through Good Dye Young.

The principles of Good Dye Young are based on self-expression and inclusivity. Because she understood that hair color is more than a fad and can represent a person's identity, Hayley created the company with a broad spectrum of people in mind. Her dedication to sustainability and her clients' well-being is evident in the high-quality ingredients used in the product formulation. Every shade has a purpose behind its name, frequently drawn from Hayley's personal experiences and the feelings she wants to portray. This deliberate strategy gives the brand a more intimate feel that appeals to followers who recognize elements of Hayley's journey in each hue.

Through her promotion of Good Dye Young, Hayley has fostered a creative and accepting community. She inspires her audience to embrace individuality and express themselves through bold hair colors through social media campaigns, tutorials, and influencer collaborations. The brand's concept is straightforward: everyone should be confident to defy social standards and take risks. By doing this, Hayley promotes a welcoming atmosphere where people from various backgrounds can unite to celebrate their uniqueness.

Another factor contributing to Good Dye Young's success is its genuine marketing strategy. Hayley interacts personally with her audience instead of merely depending on conventional advertising. She invites followers to accompany her on her path of self-discovery by sharing updates on her hair color changes. Because of her openness, she has gained a devoted following of people who genuinely relate to her aim and narrative. Hayley demonstrates the transformational potential of hair color, reinforcing the notion that self-expression can play a critical role in mental health and overall well-being.

Moreover, Hayley's impact on the fashion industry exceeds her hair color product range. She has worked with various businesses and designers, frequently utilizing her position to promote sustainable fashion. In an industry that is sometimes attacked for its adverse effects on the environment, she emphasizes the significance of being aware of customers by supporting eco-friendly products and ethical production techniques.

Hayley exemplifies her ideals through her commitment to sustainability, showing that creativity and accountability coexist.

Besides collaborating with Good Dye Young, Hayley has emerged as a style icon for other fashion designers, featuring on magazine covers and dressing uniquely for high-profile events. Her bold use of color and texture, which frequently combines punk aesthetics with feminine accents, defines her sense of style. This distinctive look has influenced many admirers to embrace creativity and try new things with their outfits.

Hayley's contribution to the fashion and beauty industries is about empowerment as much as individual expression. She questions the exclusivity frequently connected to these businesses by promoting the notion that beauty and fashion should be available to everybody. She stresses that finding what speaks to each individual is the key to self-expression, which is not limited to a particular style or fad.

Hayley's contributions to the fashion and cosmetics industries will have a lasting influence as she pursues her career. Good Dye Young has fostered an environment where creativity flourishes, and people are inspired to accept their true selves through her many collaborations. Hayley Williams inspires us all in this dynamic community, showing us that self-expression is a potent art that allows us to share our stories, celebrate our identities, and establish deeper connections with others.

Hayley's journey outside of music has demonstrated her capacity to cross conventions, and she has used her position to promote self-acceptance, inclusivity, and innovation. She is a true emblem of modern self-expression, whether through her daring fashion choices, dedication to sustainability, or her creative use of hair color.

Expressing Herself: Hair, Art, and Self-Identity

Hayley Williams' identity has always been deeply entwined with her self-expression, as seen in her ever-changing hairstyle, music, and personal style. Her hair has acted as a canvas for her to depict the changing story of her life, from her early days in Paramore to her endeavors as a lone artist and businesswoman.

In her teens, hair color had a role in Hayley's relationship with rebellion and self-discovery. She found herself yearning to escape from the traditional expectations of her surroundings as a child growing up in Meridian, Mississippi. She could express her uniqueness in a world that frequently seemed limited by dying her hair. With every new hue, whether a vivid orange, an electric blue, or a delicate pastel, Hayley expressed her feelings and experiences in a way her followers could genuinely understand.

This innovative use of her hair was a fundamental part of who she was, not just a matter of taste. As Hayley rose from a small-town girl to a worldwide rock sensation, her hair came to represent her journey. Every metamorphosis symbolized important turning points in her life, reflecting her personal and professional shifts. Her emotions, goals, and challenges were mirrored in vivid colors, which provided a window into her inner world. In this sense, the color of her hair started to symbolize her development as a person and an artist, and it became an essential component of her narrative.

In art, Hayley frequently matched the topics and feelings in her songs with her hairstyles. Her vivid color scheme matched the unadulterated passion of her lyrics, which often dealt with themes of empowerment, heartbreak, and anxiety. Her hair evolved into an extension of the storyline, a potent visual clue that enhanced her artistic ability, much as her songs expressed intense emotions. Because her music and appearance complemented each other so well, fans could relate to her on a deeper level because they could see her spirit reflected in her ever-changing style.

In addition, Hayley has challenged conventional notions of femininity and beauty standards via her platform. She bravely embraces her uniqueness in a field where limited notions of beauty frequently rule, inspiring her audience to follow suit. She reminds her audience that true beauty is found in being authentically oneself through her hair makeovers, which advocate authenticity and self-acceptance. This message strikes a deep chord in a society where conformity is often the norm, encouraging many people to embrace their distinctive qualities, whether in their appearance, hobbies, or life decisions.

The introduction of her hair color line, Good Dye Young, is another testament to her dedication to encouraging individuality via hair. The brand embodies her idea that choosing hair color should be an exciting and liberating experience rather than a limited option imposed by social conventions. A wide range of vivid colors are available from Good Dye Young, enabling people to experiment and express their creativity. Through her personal experiences and advice on hair care and upkeep, Hayley cultivates a community that embraces the transforming potential of hair color as a tool for self-exploration.

Hayley's creative abilities go beyond the business side and into the visual sphere, where she employs hair as a more expansive artistic expression component. Her hair is frequently the center of attention in her partnerships with stylists and photographers, producing arresting images that capture her individuality and creative vision. Her music and these images work together to create a seamless story that highlights the complexity of her identity. Her hair is a conscious choice that supports her personal and artistic ethos; thus, the artistry behind it goes beyond simple aesthetics.

Hayley's investigation of hair and identity speaks to the universal human condition as she develops. She inspires others to embrace their genuine selves by acting as a light of hope in a society where people frequently struggle with self-acceptance. Her experience serves as a reminder that our identities are intricate and multidimensional, molded by the stories we tell, the decisions we make, and our experiences.

Hayley frequently talks about the value of mental health in interviews and public settings, incorporating her experiences with sadness and anxiety into her story of accepting herself. She understands that choosing a new hair color and style can be a big part of self-care, giving people a chance to rediscover who they are in the face of obstacles in life. Many people view hair changes as symbolic acts of empowerment that allow them to reclaim control during difficult times. Hayley gives her admirers a sense of power in a world that may be overwhelming by being transparent about her mental health journey and encouraging them to use their hair as a tool for self-expression and healing.

Ultimately, Hayley Williams's investigation into hair, art, and self-identity proves the transformational potential of individual expression. Her experience exemplifies how people can use hair for personal storytelling to express their feelings and experiences. She encourages others to embrace their uniqueness by embracing it herself, which promotes acceptance and innovation in society. Hayley's message is crystal apparent in a society where conformity is frequently pushed since authenticity is the height of beauty and self-expression is a potent catalyst for realizing and accepting oneself.

CHAPTER 7: ADVOCACY AND INFLUENCE

Mental Health Awareness: Speaking Out for Others

With her platform, Hayley Williams has become a prominent voice in mental health discourse, advocating for more excellent knowledge and awareness of the difficulties many people encounter and sharing her personal experiences. Despite having a very personal experience navigating the problems of anxiety and depression, she has managed to turn her challenges into a source of empowerment and strength for others. Hayley wants to de-stigmatize mental health concerns by being transparent about them and starting a conversation that invites openness and support.

Fans responded favorably to Hayley's openness about her mental health when she was interviewed and engaged on social media. She underlined that mental health issues are not a sign of weakness but rather a natural part of the human experience as she described her problems. In a world where many people still struggle with the stigma associated with mental illness, this viewpoint is essential. Fans can now talk openly about their challenges in a safe area thanks to Hayley's willingness to share her tale, which has helped build a community among people who might otherwise feel alone in their experiences.

Hayley has also directly addressed issues related to mental health in her music. Songs like "Told You So" and "Fake Happy" from Paramore's "After Laughter" examine the façade many people put on to hide their inner agony. Listeners who can connect to the pressure to be "fine" even when they're not feeling fine will find resonance in these tracks. Hayley's lyrics act as a mirror, reflecting the pressures placed on society that may aggravate mental health conditions. She affirms her audience's feelings by tackling these subjects in her work and motivates them to prioritize their mental health and get treatment when necessary.

Hayley has used her social media platform to raise awareness about mental health resources in addition to her songs. She regularly publishes posts promoting self-care routines, therapy, and the value of getting professional assistance. She contributes to removing obstacles that keep many people from getting the support they need by normalizing these conversations. She frequently emphasizes the importance of mental health in her speeches, telling her audience to take care of themselves and understand that asking for assistance is a show of strength rather than weakness.

With the debut of her solo effort "Petals for Armor" in 2020, Hayley solidified her position as a mental health champion even further by fusing intimate tales about her battles with anxiety and despair. The album evolved into a therapeutic examination of her road to recovery, highlighting the difficulties of managing mental health while in the public eye. Her openness in addressing these subjects struck a deep chord, sparking more conversations about mental health within and outside the music industry.

Hayley has additionally participated in several mental health campaigns, working with groups emphasizing support, advocacy, and awareness. She collaborates with these organizations to promote their resources and messaging to people who might not otherwise be interested in discussing mental health. Her dedication to activism goes beyond raising awareness; she actively works to alter how society perceives and treats mental health.

Her advocacy for mental health has a significant impact on young people, many of whom are dealing with pressures that are never seen in today's environment. Anxiety and feelings of inadequacy might result from social media interaction, academic expectations, and cultural standards. Hayley's desire to be open and honest about her challenges provides a quick check for those who might feel overwhelmed. She stresses the value of surrounding oneself with a supportive environment and exemplifies that it's acceptable not to be okay.

In addition, Hayley uses her artistic expression as a means of self- and fan-healing. Her ability to compose music that speaks to the intricacies of mental health allows her to establish a shared experience that strengthens bonds. Supporters frequently talk about how her songs got them through their worst moments, demonstrating the significant influence of her honesty. Through her ability to express her anguish, perplexity, and hope, Hayley breaks down the stigma associated with mental health issues by making listeners feel seen and understood.

In interviews, Hayley stated that she wants to serve as a ray of hope for people going through comparable struggles. She is aware of the power of her voice and uses it to push for increased awareness and compassion for mental health. She takes her responsibility seriously, knowing that what she says might significantly affect her audience. Her genuineness and openness to vulnerability foster an atmosphere that encourages people to come forward with their struggles and ask for assistance.

Hayley Williams continues to play a critical role in the campaign as public awareness of mental health issues rises. Her experience serves as a reminder that recovery from mental health issues is achievable and that these problems are common. She fosters an environment of understanding and support by dismantling barriers and promoting candid communication. Hayley encourages people to prioritize their mental health and accept their journey toward healing through her advocacy, music, and per
sonal experiences.

Supporting Equality: LGBTQ+ Advocacy and Social Justice

Hayley Williams has made a name for herself as a formidable musical artist and a fervent supporter of social justice and LGBTQ+ rights. She is a source of inspiration and hope for many because of her unwavering dedication to equality and inclusivity, ingrained in her identity as an artist and public person.

Within the Paramore fan community, Hayley has promoted inclusivity since the beginning of her career. She has long supported the notion that everyone may feel secure in music, regardless of identity or background. The band's concerts, which are well-known for their friendly vibe, reflect this belief. Hayley's attitude to inclusivity is not just a show; it's a fundamental principle guiding her relationship with her audience and her creative process.

Hayley has significantly impacted LGBTQ+ campaigning with her outspoken support of marriage equality. She used her platform to speak out against prejudice and publicly aired her views at a time when the topic was hotly contested and discussed in the US. Her bravery inspired her followers and served as a role model for other musicians in the field. Hayley has continuously emphasized the value of acceptance and love, stating that everyone has the right to love openly and without fear of retaliation.

Besides her advocacy for marriage equality, Hayley has demonstrated unwavering support during other LGBTQ+ rights movements. Her commitment to promoting mental health resources and support networks for LGBTQ+ kids is shown by her involvement in Pride events and her outspoken support of groups like The Trevor Project. Hayley is particularly passionate about the Trevor Project's focus on crisis intervention and suicide prevention for young LGBTQ+ people. She raises awareness of the difficulties LGBTQ+ kids encounter, especially in potentially unaccepting communities, by supporting such programs.

Beyond her words in public, Hayley is involved with LGBTQ+ issues. She demonstrates her dedication to elevating different voices by actively promoting

LGBTQ+ artists, causes, and campaigns on social media. In an industry where representation is frequently lacking, this outreach is essential. She fosters an atmosphere that honors and respects many identities by highlighting the work of LGBTQ+ creators, inspiring her audience to embrace a more expansive definition of inclusion and community.

Furthermore, Hayley advocates for social justice on various problems impacting oppressed communities, not only LGBTQ+ rights. Knowing these societal concerns are linked, she has utilized her position to promote gender equality, mental health awareness, and racial equality. She has emphasized the significance of intersectionality in activism in several insightful articles and interviews, realizing that the struggle for equality must consider multiple facets of identity. Her activism is strengthened by this all-encompassing strategy, which also inspires her audience to embrace a broader definition of social justice.

In periods of social unrest, Hayley has not held back when speaking her mind. She raises awareness and demands action on issues of institutional racism, police brutality, and the continuous struggle for LGBTQ+ rights through her voice. Her readiness to discuss contentious subjects shows that she is aware of the obligations that come with celebrity. Hayley encourages her fans to become informed, get involved in the community, and donate to groups that work to bring about change. Her assertiveness empowers her audience and inspires them to become change agents in their communities.

Hayley's influence may also be seen in her partnerships with other musicians who are as dedicated to social justice as she is. Through her collaborations with musicians who support equality, she furthers the notion that art can be a potent vehicle for activism. These partnerships frequently produce music that stimulates listeners to think deeply about social concerns and have thought-provoking conversations in addition to being entertaining. Hayley demonstrates the power of unity via her artistic collaborations, demonstrating the necessity of group action in pursuing justice.

Hayley's advocacy is also informed by the relationships she has built with LGBTQ+ people in her personal life. She expands her comprehension of underprivileged populations' difficulties by surrounding herself with various viewpoints. These relationships enhance her activism and artistic abilities, enabling her to tackle problems with sincerity and empathy. Because Hayley truly cares about others, her activism profoundly impacts those who look up to her.

Hayley Williams personifies that artists must use their platforms for good through her steadfast advocacy of social justice and LGBTQ+ rights. Her dedication to diversity, activism, and consciousness gives her followers a feeling of community and inspires them to own their identities and defend their convictions. Her voice is still essential to the ongoing discussion about equality as she develops as an artist. She encourages countless people to take up the cause of a more equitable and inclusive society.

CHAPTER 8: THE EVOLUTION OF PARAMORE

"After Laughter": A New Sound, A New Era

The album "After Laughter," which Hayley Williams and Paramore published in 2017, signaled a significant change in the group's style, sound, and thematic focus. "After Laughter" introduced a new musical palette, moving away from their previous albums' darker, more angst-driven music. It was full of pop-influenced melodies, new-wave overtones, and a moving contrast between cheerful sounds and reflective lyrics. This change represented the band's development and Hayley's changing self as a person and artist, offering a rich canvas for investigation.

Renowned producer Justin Meldal-Johnsen, who had previously collaborated with the band on their "Paramore" album, helped to create the record. He significantly impacted the development of the new sound "After Laughter." The group adopted a more avant-garde style, adding rhythmic grooves that evoked the sounds of the 1980s and layering synths. This change in sound allowed Paramore to carve out a distinct place for themselves in the modern music world while simultaneously drawing comparisons to legendary pop acts of that era. This new direction was demonstrated by songs like "Hard Times" and "Told You So," which combined popular rhythms with lyrics that explored existential themes of vulnerability and fear.

The joyful instrumentation on the record contrasted sharply with its reflective themes. Although the songs had unquestionably catchy melodies, the lyrics provided an open window into Hayley's issues, such as her bouts with melancholy and anxiety. "Hard Times," the album's lead single, establishes the mood with its upbeat melody, but the lyrics also discuss emotions of hopelessness and the need to keep up a happy front. The core of "After Laughter" is embodied by this dichotomy, which highlights the complexity of human emotion and the frequently hidden hardships behind a happy façade.

Writing "After Laughter" was a very intimate songwriting process for Hayley as she dealt with her mental health issues. She could express situations many listeners could identify with through the record, which turned into a cathartic investigation of her emotions. Songs like "Fake Happy," which capture the sensation of detachment that may accompany social expectations, frankly confront the temptation to fake happiness. Fans were moved by Hayley's willingness to be open and honest in her lyrics since it gave people going through similar things a voice. Through this link, listeners felt more connected to one another and sought comfort in their common difficulties with mental health.

"After Laughter" had a vivid, bright visual style that complemented its upbeat musical style. The beautiful images from the album artwork showed Hayley frequently dressed in colorful, creative costumes that exuded a spirit of exploration and freedom. This new visual identity represented a new chapter in the band's history and changed from the darker tones of previous albums. This concept was carried in the accompanying music videos, which were released in conjunction with the album and featured whimsical and surreal visuals in contrast to the deeper emotional storylines expressed in the lyrics of songs like "Told You So" and "Rose-Colored Boy." These images contributed to the recognition of "After Laughter" as a multifaceted piece of art that combined fashion, music, and individual expression.

Widespread critical acclaim greeted "After Laughter"'s release, with many applauding the band's daring and willingness to try new sounds. With its debut at number six on the Billboard 200, the album cemented Paramore's standing in the contemporary music scene. Its commercial success further reflected the band's progression from the pop-punk roots that first defined their career to a more diverse and mature sound. This change invited fans from different genres to interact with the band's music and created opportunities for new audiences.

In addition, Hayley used "After Laughter" as a forum to discuss mental health and emotional well-being in more general talks. She addressed the album's inspiration in interviews and promotional events, stressing the value of being transparent about mental health concerns. By doing this, she upheld her mental health awareness advocate position and urged her listeners to prioritize their well-being. Hayley's dedication to openness and genuineness defined her not just as a performer but also as an inspiration for people facing comparable difficulties.

Fans found great resonance in the album's themes of self-acceptance and resiliency, which helped to rebuild the band's relationship with their fanbase. Thanks to Hayley's openness to share her stories, many listeners took solace in knowing they were not alone in their troubles. This sense of community was essential when conversations about mental health were becoming more popular. "After Laughter" added to this conversation by providing realistic stories that promoted openness and transparency.

The band's live performances turned into a celebration of the themes from the album as they started their promotion tour for "After Laughter." Concertgoers were moved by Hayley's enthusiasm on stage and the catchy melodies of the new songs, which combined to create an upbeat environment. Fans of "After Laughter" sang along, comprehending the deeper meanings of the lyrics, making the songs become anthems for individuals navigating their emotional landscapes. The band's relationship with its fans cemented Paramore's position as a voice for a generation struggling with mental health and their status as musicians.

Hayley has kept thinking back on the significance of the record and the journey it represented in the years after "After Laughter" was released. Her artistic development reached a new height with this undertaking, proving she could change and develop without losing her identity. The album's themes are still relevant today as a gentle reminder to listeners of the value of vulnerability, self-compassion, and the never-ending quest for mental health.

The Bond with Bandmates: Changing Dynamics

Hayley Williams's relationship with her Paramore band mates has been a complicated tapestry of shifting dynamics and a source of strength throughout her career. These friendships have influenced the music they make and each other's paths as friends and musicians from the beginning of their creation to the present.

Bassist Jeremy Davis, brothers Zac and Josh Farro, and Hayley made up the original lineup of Paramore in 2004. There was a youthful exuberance and vitality to this first lineup, which fostered an environment that encouraged invention. Although lead singer Hayley frequently stole the show, there was a clear sense of teamwork among the band members. A typical enthusiasm marked their early rehearsals for creating music, as they blended rock, pop, and punk influences to create a sound that connected with their fellow musicians. The relationships that would both strengthen and test them in the years to come were established by this early camaraderie.

The demands of the music business started to put their relationships to the test as Paramore gained popularity and started touring. There were difficulties involved in going from being local musicians to international celebrities. The ongoing obligations of recording, touring, and public appearances strain the band's dynamics. The first rush of achievement progressively gave way to a more complicated reality where conflicts between the artistic and personal selves started to show. Being the front woman meant Hayley had to balance her creative vision and her bandmates' demands and wants. This delicate balancing effort frequently called for tough talks and concessions.

The band's self-titled album release in 2013 was one of the turning points in their existence. The band saw significant changes during this time due to the departure of original members Josh Farro and Zac. Their departure was a game-changer, forcing Hayley and the other band members—Taylor York and Zac Farro's brother, among others—to reevaluate their relationships and reinterpret their respective roles in the group. For Hayley, losing longtime friends and partners was more than a personal tragedy; it was a significant time for reflection. As she reflected on their shared experiences and memories, she realized that their relationship would have to change for them to go on.

Following these adjustments, Hayley concentrated on fostering her relationship with Taylor York, who had served as a close confidante and collaborator. Their partnership grew as they worked through the uncertainty of a changing music scene. A new creative synergy resulted from this dynamic shift, as Hayley and Taylor started to venture into unexplored musical territory together. They could push limits and try out new sounds since they respected one another's artistic abilities. The direction of "After Laughter" was greatly influenced by this revitalized sense of teamwork, as they each contributed their unique skills to produce something original and creative.

Hayley learned more and more during this time of transition about the value of mental and emotional wellness, not only for herself but also for her bandmates. Relationships often suffer from the demands of celebrity, but Hayley deliberately worked to encourage candid communication within the group. She ensured that everyone in the band felt heard and appreciated by enabling them to talk about their emotions. This dedication to emotional openness was essential to the band's ability to overcome obstacles as a unit and to reestablish confidence and togetherness.

Not only did the relationships within Paramore change throughout time, but Hayley's leadership did, too. She accepted that teamwork is more than just playing music;

it also entails fostering an atmosphere where everyone may succeed. This method fostered a feeling of community, giving each band member the confidence to share their distinct viewpoints. Live performances showcased the growing chemistry between Hayley and her bandmates, as their combined energy produced a captivating stage presence. Fans had an incredible experience due to the group's genuine connection, which was palpable to the audience.

Hayley's devotion to her bandmates grew as time went on, going beyond only music. She realized that they were family, not simply partners in crime. The everyday triumphs and tragedies created strong relationships that extended beyond the theater. Interviews revealed this familial link, as Hayley frequently discussed the value of these connections openly and honestly. She underlined that even though the music business can be tricky, having a solid support network is crucial. The band overcame difficulties thanks to their cohesiveness, strengthening their belief that they could weather any storm as a group.

Hayley's analysis of Paramore's dynamics has become more complex in recent years as the band has expanded and changed. She agreed that change is an inevitable aspect of any relationship, particularly in a band setting. The respect and understanding they had developed over the years held steadfast despite occasional arguments or divergent viewpoints. Hayley frequently reflected on the lessons she had gained from negotiating these difficulties, realizing that setbacks and victories are pieces of their journey's larger story.

CHAPTER 9: LIFE IN PROGRESS

Navigating Her 30s: Reflections on Growth and Change

When Hayley Williams turned thirty, she started a path of self-discovery, reflection, and significant change. This decade in her life turned out to be crucial for both her creative and personal development. Hayley's thirty-first birthday acted as a wake-up call in many respects, forcing her to reassess her life, identity, and work and face the challenges of maturity head-on with vulnerability and bravery.

At first, Hayley was a little nervous and excited about turning thirty. Social pressures and expectations are typically associated with reaching a milestone birthday, especially for women in the music business. In a society that frequently values youth, many artists find it difficult to age, creating an internal conflict between one's authenticity and the public's views. But instead of giving in to these demands, Hayley accepted her age as a virtue. She realized that all of her experiences—both positive and negative—had molded her into the person and artist she is today.

Deep introspection was a defining feature of this stage of her life. Hayley started to think back on her decisions and routes to get to this point. She was forced to reflect on her values after encountering difficulties in her personal and professional lives. She was open in interviews about how her views on celebrity, achievement, and the effects of her mental health issues have changed over time. She discovered that the story of success was frequently constrained and oversimplified, concentrating only on tangible accomplishments. Instead, she sought a more complex explanation that included emotional health, genuineness, and interpersonal relationships.

Hayley's increasing focus on raising awareness of mental health issues was critical to this journey. Although her experiences with anxiety and sadness had influenced her artistic work, she felt compelled to take up the cause of mental health advocacy on a larger scale as she approached her 30s. She started talking candidly about her difficulties to de-stigmatize these discussions inside and outside the music industry. Fans responded well to her willingness to share her journey; many found comfort in her honesty. Because of Hayley's honesty, others were inspired to prioritize their mental health and get help.

In addition, Hayley experienced a significant change in her relationship with her music during this time. She found herself thinking back on the development of Paramore's sound and her creative identity following the publication of "After Laughter." The album's success and the difficulties she encountered while making it inspired her to pursue new artistic endeavors. This investigation was about more than just experimenting with music; it was also about finding her voice again as a solo performer. Hayley started to embrace the concept of artistic autonomy after realizing that she could express herself freely from the limitations imposed by band dynamics.

Her newly discovered independence resulted from her solo effort, "Petals for Armor." Her journey is reflected in the album, which captures her maturation and the lessons she discovered in her 30s. Hayley explored love, grief, empowerment, and self-acceptance themes in each song. She was able to reclaim her story by making this music, expressing her experiences with genuineness and unfiltered emotion. By doing this, she created a stronger bond with her listeners by allowing them to see how she has changed.

The images accompanying "Petals for Armor" similarly depicted this stage of Hayley's development. The eye-catching hues, imaginative images, and provocative subjects demonstrated her openness to change and her desire to express herself uniquely. Her artistic decisions for the album's packaging demonstrated her aim to dispel stereotypes about what it meant to be a successful thirty-something female singer. With the help of her platform, Hayley broke stereotypes and argued that growing older in the music business can be a positive and empowering experience.

Hayley negotiated her relationships and connections with a fresh sense of purpose. She tackled these situations with a feeling of realism, understanding that the complexity of adulthood frequently calls for challenging conversations and choices. She understood the significance of surrounding herself with those who encouraged and supported her personal development, whether via sexual relationships or friendships. This emphasis on healthy connections enhanced her entire feeling of contentment, which made it possible for her to embrace intimacy and vulnerability sincerely.

Hayley's dedication to social justice and campaigning was crucial to her 30-year-old journey. She utilized her voice to advocate for causes near and dear to her heart as she became more conscious of the structural problems that underprivileged populations face. She participated in conversations on mental health, equality, and the value of representation in the arts, in addition to her musical career. Her commitment to social justice strengthened her position as a thought leader in the music business and demonstrated that musicians can use their power for good.

In this decade of her life, Hayley also embraced the concept of self-care as a critical discipline for sustaining her mental and emotional wellness. She looked into several ways to learn about herself, such as mindfulness, counseling, and artistic pursuits outside of music. Through the chaos of her profession, she had previously been illusive of a sense of calm and balance, but this comprehensive approach helped her to reconnect with herself. Hayley set an example for her fans by putting self-care first and showing them how important it is to look after oneself in a society with high expectations.

Hayley Williams revealed herself as a more grounded, genuine person when she reflected on her journey through her 30s—someone who faced life's challenges with grit and grace. Her challenges became essential to her story, enhancing her artistic vision and strengthening her bond with her audience. This period of her life turned into a potent illustration of the idea that personal development is a continuous process resulting from every encounter, connection, and self-realization.

Future Aspirations: What's Next for Hayley?

Hayley Williams sees a world of boundless opportunities ahead of her as she considers her journey via music, personal development, and social action. Her goals for the future are more than just lofty goals; they are intricately linked to the changes in her identity, values, and life lessons. As she enters a new career stage, Hayley is ready to pursue creative endeavors, increase her influence on social concerns, and redefine what it means to be a successful artist in the modern world.

Hayley hopes to carry out more independent artistic development in the near future. She is eager to explore her musicianship after "Petals for Armor" achieved critical and commercial success. This journey is about pushing limits and embracing innovation, not just making new music. Hayley has stated that she wants to work across genres and styles with various musicians. Her willingness to work together reflects her conviction that many viewpoints and influences enhance creativity. Listeners may anticipate a combination of sounds that push conventional boundaries as she embarks on new projects, allowing them to experience her constantly changing aural universe.

Hayley is committed to pursuing her advocacy work and her musical pursuits, especially in social justice, equality, and mental health. Acknowledging her position as a public person, she wants to use her power to spread awareness and bring about change. Hayley hopes to work with community-based groups, support programs that strengthen underprivileged communities, and give voice to those frequently ignored. She believes that artists must contribute to essential topics, and her dedication to using her platform for good is a pillar of her future goals.

Hayley also understands the need for mental health advocacy, especially in the music industry, where there are sometimes a lot of pressures and inflated expectations. She wants to start forums and workshops to encourage mental wellness in both fans and artists. Hayley aims to dispel the stigma associated with mental health concerns by establishing secure forums for candid conversation, thereby cultivating a supportive and empathetic community. In her ideal world, mental health would be valued as a personal issue and a group duty within the music industry.

Regarding personal development, Hayley is dedicated to continuous self-exploration. She has discussed how therapy and mindfulness can change a person's life and intends to prioritize these activities. This dedication to self-care is a fundamental change in her perspective on well-being, not merely a fad. Hayley understands that personal development is a lifetime endeavor, and she plans to embrace each stage with sincerity and intention. Through her experiences, she wants to encourage people to start their journeys of self-discovery.

As a creative who has negotiated the challenges of notoriety and media attention, Hayley knows how crucial authenticity will be to her future aspirations. Her goal is to produce art that genuinely connects and invites contemplation from her viewers. Her aspiration for authenticity goes beyond music; she sees herself creating content for various platforms, such as literature and visual art. To bring her audience into her world in novel and fascinating ways, Hayley strives to investigate the intersections of art and personal experience through essays, poetry, and visual storytelling.

Hayley is also eager to investigate the relationship between music and fashion. She sees the possibility for creative expression beyond the musical stage with her bold wardrobe choices and unique style. To produce collections that reflect her artistic vision and connect with her audience, Hayley has indicated an interest in working with fashion designers and businesses who share her ideals. She wants to spread a message of individualism and self-expression by challenging conventional standards of beauty and style through her endeavors.

Hayley is ambitious about international tours outside conventional music venues on a bigger stage. Her idea involves small-scale exhibitions in non-traditional venues such as community centers, art galleries, and outdoor areas, emphasizing interpersonal relationships and shared experiences. Her method reflects her conviction that music is a universal language that unites people from all origins and cultures. Her goal in designing these distinctive spaces is to encourage community and belonging among her followers.

CONCLUSION

Considering the diverse legacy Hayley Williams is leaving behind as we end her incredible adventure is essential. Hayley's tale is one of tenacity, sincerity, and creative integrity. It starts with her upbringing in Meridian, Mississippi, and continues with her ascent to prominence as Paramore's lead singer and activist. Her life is a perfect example of the struggles and victories musicians face and the significant influence one person can have on a whole generation.

Hayley has shown grace and tenacity in navigating the frequently turbulent seas of the music industry throughout her career. She has struggled with mental health issues, personal loss, and stardom, and she has used these experiences as inspiration for her work. Whether she's released it as a solo artist or with Paramore, every record demonstrates her honesty and maturity. By letting her fans into her world and revealing both the light and the shadows within her, Hayley has shown her heart to them via her lyrics. Because of her openness, she has developed a close bond with her audience that goes beyond simple amusement to serve as a source of inspiration and solace for many people.

Hayley's impact goes beyond just her songs. She has become a crucial voice in discussions about mental health, promoting awareness and comprehension in a field that frequently ignores the psychological costs of celebrity. In addition to de-stigmatizing these problems, her willingness to talk about her troubles has inspired others to get help and be honest about their experiences. By doing this, Hayley has empowered her followers to put their well-being first and support one another, turning her struggles into a movement.

Furthermore, Hayley's dedication to equality and social justice says a lot about her character. She has continuously promoted LGBTQ+ rights, mental health awareness, and other social causes using her platform. She has become a role model for young musicians and a ray of light for people striving for acceptance and equality by integrating her artistic vision with her moral principles. Hayley's activism draws attention to music's ability as a vehicle for social change and serves as a reminder that musicians can and ought to interact with their surroundings.

Hayley Williams finds herself at a turning point in her career where her activism and artistic endeavors converge. As she continues to push the boundaries of her profession, she has new musical undertakings, collaborations, and creative excursions in mind. Her ambition reflects her desire to significantly contribute to culture rather than just her pursuit of personal success. She pledges that every new endeavor will reflect her progress, learnings, and experiences to keep her artistic path fresh and exciting.

Hayley Williams is the embodiment of progress. She is an artist who values genuineness, accepts change, and honors individuality. Her experience serves as a reminder that progress is not linear but consists of many peaks and troughs that all add to the intricate fabric of life. She continues to motivate people to embrace their paths and face obstacles head-on with bravery and resiliency as she negotiates the complexity of maturity.

Hayley Williams left a legacy of connection, empowerment, and creative talent. She represents what it means to be authentic in a society that frequently encourages conformity. Hayley has forged a career that distinguishes her as a singular artist and inspires others around her via her music, activism, and genuine human connection. Her influence will undoubtedly last for years as she keeps growing, encouraging upcoming generations to accept their unique identities and follow their passions with unflinching tenacity. Hayley Williams is a talented musician and a force to be reckoned with, a role model, and an example of the value of openness and sincerity in the arts and everyday life.

Printed in Great Britain
by Amazon

53376267R00073